POSTER GIRL HABITS

Creating an Intentional Contentment Practice

Enjoy your life ♡

Kim Smith

WRITTEN BY KIM SMITH

An Unbelievable Freedom Book

*Those who flow as life flows know
they need no other force.*

LAO TZU

DEDICATION

I dedicate this book to my husband, Ryan. I am grateful for his investment in my contentment since the beginning. Ryan, thank you for supporting and encouraging my Poster Girl Flow.

ACKNOWLEDGMENT

I want to thank Eled Cernik for designing covers for all four Unbelievable Freedom books. It's been an unbelievably productive year and I couldn't have done it without you!

Table of Contents

Introduction

Welcome, Contentment Seekers.

I'm Kim Smith, author of the Unbelievable Freedom Books. The one you're holding is the newest, and like the others, it's related to the five-year transformation that rendered me unrecognizable. This book condenses the most important changes I've made into a set of actionable steps called Poster Girl Habits. Layered together, they create my Intentional Contentment Practice. This book exists to encourage you in developing a contentment practice of your own.

A couple of things to bear in mind throughout: first, contentment isn't limited to people who are highly evolved or incredibly disciplined or super spiritual. Contentment is for people who choose to practice and channel it. I hope that's what you'll do as we flow through this practice together.

Second, contentment isn't something a person is born with; it's something they choose. Though I didn't experience it for a lot of my life, it's something I've intentionally cultivated in recent years. Contentment is for everyone, so contentment is for YOU.

WHO is the Poster Girl for Contentment? I am. You may or may not be familiar with my story. Suffice it to say that I used to be a deeply discontented, self-pitying person. Moving out of that mindset and into my current way of being was a revelation. As I became more peaceful and joyful, I barely recognized myself. One day I said, "I feel like I should be the Poster Girl for Contentment," and I've claimed it since that moment.

WHAT are Poster Girl Habits? They are the practices I engage in daily to stay in a state of contentment. I didn't invent anything here - I didn't discover appreciation, mindfulness, gratitude, or positive self-talk. However, what I've done is gathered and organized an accessible, whimsical system. I also refer to my Poster Girl Habits as the "The 5 E's" and the list below shows why.

❯ Habit 1: ENERGY
  Outcome: Wellness of Body

❯ Habit 2: EXPECTATION
  Outcome: Lightness of Mind

❯ Habit 3: EASY DELIGHTS
  Outcome: Brightness of Mood

❯ Habit 4: EVERYDAY RITUALS
  Outcome: Depth of Satisfaction

❯ Habit 5: EDITING
  Outcome: Enjoyment of Life

Lastly, what is this thing I'm referring to as Poster Girl Flow? It's living life from a contented place almost all the time. It's difficult to be wrenched out of that flow, and if you're consistently practicing The Habits, it's easy to get back in. I refer throughout this book to layering the Habits because each one flows into the next.

I stay in Poster Girl Flow seven days a week, morning, noon, and night. The times that I get out of flow are rare, and when I do, I'm aware and immediately cued to get back in. Just like I'm barely recognizable in the mirror, my current life looks almost nothing like the old one.

If you've read my previous books, you know freedom is a theme woven throughout. You know I'm on a quest to enjoy my life as part of my grandmother's legacy. If you read my Book of Contemplations called *Unmired*, you'll find these Poster Girl concepts are completely aligned with that book's message. The intent of this workbook is to move from contemplation to action!

Let's flow,

Kim

Energy

Introducing the Habit: Energy

Here we are, beginning a fresh practice with a new set of habits! I'm excited to have you take this journey with me. This is truly an invitation into the way I live every day of my life. Living this way has been unbelievable for me, and I hope it will be for you.

As usual, I'm asking you to start from a place of faith. Believe in Poster Girl Flow: that contentment is a central "way of being" in the world if we choose it and practice it. Our aim is to build a foundation of contentment for your life. Contentment was my grandmother's way of being, and she's the example after whom I modeled my own practice.

For now, let me paint a picture of what Poster Girl Habit #1 is all about. It's called ENERGY, and its outcome is WELLNESS OF BODY. What do you think of when I say the word ENERGY? For most, it's the opposite of fatigue, having enough stamina to get through the day. But in the case of ENERGY as a Poster Girl Habit, I'm talking about the vibrancy of feeling good. It's a kind of internal ENERGY that starts from (and expands out from) your physical body. It's very difficult to feel contentment in your life if your body doesn't feel good, so that is the place from which we start.

Throughout this book, I'll make reference to my "discontented life" as a way of contrasting how things used to be before my transformation. I rarely ever felt good physically. Even before my weight gain, I ate in a way that kept my body bogged down. I felt tired, achy, and generally icky a lot of the time.

Now, I feel great, pretty much all the time. I accomplish this by layering some key pieces. The first one is fasting, and though this isn't a fasting program, I wouldn't be the Poster Girl without fasting's feel-good vibes. My first Habit Creation Guide deals with fasting if that's a habit you wish to create. Whether you fast or not, you need a way to keep your body feeling good so you can practice this habit.

In addition to fasting, I maintain a healthy weight for my frame, I eat foods that fuel my body and spirit, I stay committed to an intentional walking practice, and I get plenty of sleep. These are ingredients in my ENERGY recipe, and you're going to identify yours.

Until next time, just hold this idea in your mind: feeling good is our contentment foundation, and we are going to make sure it's a solid one.

Strive to feel vibrant,

Kim

Feeling Good

We're flowing with Poster Girl Habits and I hope that you already feel a bit more contented, just having made the decision to invest in yourself this way. We're going to continue our work around ENERGY, or good vibes, and how this habit supports my contentment. When you start from a place of feeling good physically, it's easier to build contentment habits.

One technique I teach throughout this practice is asking guiding questions. I'll ask them of you, but more importantly, you'll learn to ask them of yourselves. During my transformation, I used something lovely and resonant like, "Is this choice in full alignment with my highest goals?" That's a good one, but for our purposes, let's keep it really short and sweet: "Is this a contentment-honoring choice?"

This takes practice, but I can now answer that question intuitively. Let's use the example of an opportunity to eat homemade baked goods. In that instance, sometimes the answer is yes and sometimes, it's no. It depends on the day, what's going on with my life and my body, and what aspect of my vibe needs tweaking.

Sometimes I've already had too much sugar and a cookie would make me bloated or nauseated. Other times, I could use a little lift and a lovely organic scone studded with ginger and currants fits the bill. Same item, different impact on my contentment.

So practice asking that question when faced with an opportunity to eat or not, walk or not, sleep or not. Is this a contentment-honoring choice? Will this help or harm my overarching goal to be content? This makes a decision about buying a scone less about rules or a diet, and more about maintaining my contentment flow.

For me, contentment comes from practicing all five habits, and habit one is ENERGY, or feel-good vibes. It's made so much difference in my life!

Honor contentment,

Kim

Deep Well-Being

We continue our focus on the first habit, ENERGY. Are you feeling a different level of attunement? I hope so. One central piece of my Poster Girl life is being really tuned in to my body, what it wants and what it needs.

Do you know what I mean when I describe a "blissful state of deep physical well-being"? Is it something you've experienced lately, or often? Some tell me that this is not a feeling they've experienced, and for those people, I want that fact to change.

For me, this state of well-being is most powerfully invoked by fasting, but I believe it can happen to anyone who practices the right self-care regimen for their physical body. When you've got your ENERGY regimen honed, it should be a common occurrence.

It's more than feeling good. It is deep physical contentment. For me, it starts with freedom from a variety of small physical woes. It's the sense that everything inside me is humming along harmoniously. Forgive the overused term, but it's amazing.

If you cannot relate, if you are not experiencing this phenomenon day-to-day, ask what's standing in the way. Fatigue? Digestive distress? Bloating? An inflammatory process like an allergy? Headaches or other vague aches and pains?

Teasing out what stands between you and a deep sense of well-being is important because contentment starts from living in a body that feels GOOD. Just like there is no such thing as looking perfect, there is no such thing as feeling perfect. Perfection is a myth but feeling great is my truth. Tuning in and listening to my body is the centerpiece of the Poster Girl Habit of ENERGY. Feeling great is the blank canvas we want to start painting our lives on.

As we flow forward, we will talk about two-way Body Trust as well as Body Wonder. They're additional sub-habits that build our ENERGY foundation.

Be Deeply Well,

Kim

Body Trust & Wonder

Another way I stay in body alignment is through practicing body trust and body wonder. I will break these sub-habits down separately, but in my mind, they are woven together.

Trusting my body means no longer agonizing about how a particular food I eat or a situation I enter is going to cause weight gain, illness, or problems. Many things in my journey, most notably fasting, taught me to embrace my body's capability. I know that if I choose to eat something, my body will work it out. As long as I listen for reactions, I can adjust accordingly in the future.

Letting go of fear and guilt around food helps us trust our bodies and even trust food. It invites a new ENERGY - a good one. It releases struggle, which is the aim of the entire contentment practice.

A related sub-habit is body wonder, marveling in amazement at what my body can do, how it can transform and heal. Having a lean body after being morbidly obese is the biggest contributor to my awe, but I work to channel wonder over all my body's functions.

I look at my decisions - my contentment-honoring decisions - as opportunities to support the incredible process of my body healing and rebuilding itself, day by day. The decision to fast honors my contentment, and so does choosing the right food when I eat. The more I enjoy my life, the more I want a body to live joyfully from, so I do my best to make great choices.

Next, we'll explore a bit about food and honoring our bodies - each day brings chances to do right or wrong by our bodies, but don't look at them as a set up for failure or despair. See them as possibilities for building contentment, upon which we'll layer our habits to come.

In trust and wonder,

Kim

Digestive Agreement

Another mini practice or "sub habit" for this Poster Girl is staying in digestive agreement. Simply put, our bodies (and our digestive systems) all function differently. Standard advice on caring for our bodies has behaved as though we can all operate on the same blueprint, which is simply not true.

It connects back to our ancestors, genetic diversity from our heritage, the way our bodies formed in utero, and how we were birthed and fed in our early months. There are also anatomic variations from more recent disease - some people cannot tolerate fiber due to mechanical changes from inflammatory bowel conditions. Our bodies are just not the same!

While our bodies have an awesome capacity to heal, we also must respect their physiological and structural reactions to what we take in. When you eat food that doesn't work for your body, it decreases contentment. When you eat what works well for your body, you live in a state of digestive agreement, increasing the odds of inducing that sought-after feeling of deep well-being.

Does all this mean you can't indulge on special occasions, eating foods you KNOW won't make your body feel good? No, it doesn't. Of course you can make that choice, but you do it with intentionality. You honor your overarching commitment to contentment. You make a conscious decision to go out of alignment with your body temporarily, then consciously steer yourself right back in.

We all have foods that are special to us for taste or sentimental reasons. The pleasure they bring is strong enough to be worth (briefly) inducing digestive disagreement. When contemplating what to eat, ask yourself if it's really worth it, and if it is, dive in!

This inner dialogue of questioning what and when to eat will become more intuitive as part of your Poster Girl Habit of ENERGY. This habit has made my interactions with food stress-free and joy-filled. It helps me stay in an unmired flow of contentment because I don't have to waste time or energy feeling lousy. Does this food serve my contentment goals? I always know the answer!

Stay in Agreement,

Kim

Visualizing Physical Contentment

Let's call this exercise, "My Ideal (Body) Day In the Future."

Visualization is powerful, so before we wrap up our exploration of ENERGY as a habit, we are going to walk through a bit of guided imagery. We've been getting attuned to how your body feels and the connection that ENERGY has to your overall lived experience. Now, let's do some active picturing. Every day can't be the ideal, but an ideal does just that: it sets the standard for comparison whenever your contentment habit seems to be faltering.

Usually, a guided imagery exercise starts with "Close your eyes," but please don't, it makes reading much harder! Just imagine a day when your body feels so good that it's easy to build contentment around that feeling. How do you feel when you wake up? Rested, I imagine. What else? How do you feel as you move through the day?

What and when do you eat, and how does it impact your overall feelings? I bet you feel free of aches and pains, free of digestive woes, but really imagine how that feels. Conjure up a vivid picture. Use your imagination to create the image of true physical contentment.

Compare your ideal ENERGY to how you actually feel in this moment, and it will guide you to what needs to change. Contentment isn't built on feeling hungry or restricted, nor is it layered on feeling bloated and over-indulged. It's more challenging to contend with overt symptoms like headaches or fatigue, but these can be addressed through active experimentation.

Habit #5 will be EDITING, and we will talk about creating tangible change in your life, but for now, hold the image of "ideal feels." Envision the ENERGY you want in your body, and compare your current reality to your ideal often.

Visualize body contentment,

Kim

Bringing It All Together

This brings us to the end of the introduction to Habit One, ENERGY, so let's bring it all together.

The foundation of the Poster Girl Habits is ENERGY, or feel-good vibes. I described my own recipe for physical contentment, including fasting, eating foods that are ideal for my body, consistent walking, and quality sleep. I encouraged you to develop a regimen that equally supports your feeling good. That's a work in progress, but I hope you have a solid start.

Now let's review the other sub-habits:

❯ Deep Well-Being: Striving to feel deeply well, sensations that transcend feeling 'just OK'. Deep well-being is a profound sense of harmony inside the body, and it's invoked by staying in physical contentment as much of the time as possible.

❯ Body Trust: Trusting your body and it trusting you is a two-way street. Avoiding fear-based attitudes toward the body will keep you in a state of trust. Trusting your body means you don't have to fear food or any particular situation you enter.

❯ Body Wonder: Being in a state of body wonder motivates contentment-honoring choices. It highlights the opportunity to participate in something marvelous by supporting our body's processes. Taking care of our bodies isn't something we have to do, it's something we are blessed to do.

❯ Digestive Agreement: While dieting isn't a Poster Girl Habit, identifying and eating foods that work best for the body supports the flow. The more we craft the right mix, the deeper the sense of wellness. And eating foods we find pleasurable adds to contentment in totally obvious ways!

I hope you are seeing how physical contentment creates that canvas on which we'll layer the subsequent Poster Girl Habits. Up next, Habit Two: EXPECTATION!

Expect contentment,

Kim

Expectation

Introducing the Habit: Expectation

While holding in mind that ENERGY is our foundational Poster Girl Habit, believing we need a body that feels good to take the next step, let's flow forward. The second habit is EXPECTATION, and its outcome is LIGHTNESS OF MIND.

EXPECTATION is the word I use to capture the Poster Girl mindset. The word itself calls up the anticipation you feel when you wake in the morning with an amazing day ahead of you. As the Poster Girl, I expect to enjoy all my days. It's the story that over-wrote the old one, the one that expected discontentment. As I'm about to step out the door to face the day, I don't know what it will hold, but I know I'll be content.

Because our thoughts and our emotions are linked, it stands to reason that thoughts of positive (expectant) thoughts = positive feelings. This mindset didn't come naturally; it's a habit I practiced and now a habit I'll teach you. There are a few key aspects of this habit and we will break them down one at a time.

I'm sure you've heard of using affirmations or "positive self-talk." That is what this habit is based upon, but I never found success using them in isolation. Being mired in a lousy day - or a discontented life - cannot be reset by simply looking in a mirror and saying, "You got this, girl!" or some other cliched mantra.

The EXPECTATION habit is more intentional, more systematic than that. It's developing a solid expectation that things will go well and letting that story be the one you tell as you live your life. The more you tell yourself that story with sincere belief, the more you witness it coming true. Again, how do I know? I've lived it the past five years. It proves itself to me over and over.

It's knowing that when "stuff happens", things that don't fit your personal model of Enjoy-Your-Life, you are empowered to change the situation (more on that at the end!). It's feeling capable and free, not trapped and stifled.

So, while continuing to practice ENERGY, look ahead to how we can use EXPECTATION - expecting to be content - to build another floor on top of our foundation.

Rewrite your story,

Kim

Self Talk Shapes Things

I have this picture taken for a website photoshoot. I'm smiling a serene smile, holding a large mug in both hands - it's a visual image of the story I tell about myself: I'm someone contented, someone who knows what she likes, someone who enjoys her life.

This story so different than the one I told a few years ago. My old story went something like this: I'm someone who struggles, I eat poorly, I have little willpower around food, my jobs haven't worked out, I can't seem to make friends, I don't enjoy anything enough to call it a hobby, etc. It's a story that makes me sad to this day, years later.

Even then, I could (on my own or with help) reframe those things more positively when I stepped back from the narrative. If someone pointed out that I was smart, caring, articulate, a great mom, I could see it. But left to my own devices, I always went back to telling that same old story.

That story led to an EXPECTATION that things would not work out. I did not expect to enjoy my moments. I did not expect to enjoy my life. I was on the lookout for negativity and I saw it everywhere. That is, ultimately, what my grandmother saw that inspired her fateful words, "Enjoy Your Life!" She could see I was letting my days pass me by. My life had great contentment potential, but I didn't see it because I was playing an old tape over and over.

So ask yourself this, what tape are you playing? What story are you telling about your life? What EXPECTATION does it create for how you feel moment-to-moment or day-to-day? I hope it isn't as dismal as mine was, but take a moment to honestly identify it. The self talk shapes the story, and the story is everything.

The EXPECTATION habit is built brick-by-brick by identifying the story and starting to rewrite it. It plays so automatically that we sometimes don't even hear it, but we are going to start to listen closely. Once we know what it is, we can flip it so that it fits our flow.

Rewrite your story,

Kim

Monitoring Old Narratives

Building that EXPECTATION habit, what story did you identify yesterday? This would be a great moment to jot down over on the notes side - even a snippet of the old story. Can you see connections between it playing as an automatic tape, and how you feel? Does the story poise your EXPECTATION for contentment....or something else?

I wrote this Contentment Creation Guide as a tool for people who have lost (or never found) their own contentment, so I know there's a chance that your old story is a fully happy or pretty one. I understand the strong odds that your narrative is setting you up to feel discontent on some level.

Flowing forward, let's practice catching ourselves telling the old version. Work to really stay in contentment, feeling it hour by hour so that you'll be keenly aware when the flow is disrupted. When discontentment comes over you - when negative emotions begin swirling - try to play back the most recent tape by a few seconds.

Do you know that 30-second rewind you can hit on a podcast or audiobook? Hit the virtual equivalent of that. When you catch the old story coming up, A HA, make a note of some kind. Again, it's great to jot a written note, but even a mental one starts to disrupt the pattern. If you're listening to an ugly, old story that is throwing you off course, you want to look directly at it. Don't run from or avoid it, see it for what it is so that you recognize it whenever it tries to creep back in.

When you identify the old story, remember the new story. It's a really easy one. The story for your life now is this: "I expect contentment." The longer version is that you expect contentment because it's possible, you're capable of it, and you're deserve every bit.

More contentment to come,

Kim

On Worthiness & Limiting Beliefs

Now that we've done some work to identify the old narrative, it's time to dig a bit deeper. Some of these patterns are deep grooves, ones so rutted that we may not be able to smooth them out. Even if we can't, raising our awareness makes it possible to navigate around them. As always, I speak from experience.

I'm going to tell you a story about what Brene Brown calls a "shame spiral." Part of my old narrative is about myself as someone unsuccessful, particularly in my career/finances. As multiple professional paths led to dead ends, I adopted a belief that I didn't have a successful career because I didn't deserve one. I've done a huge amount of work to rewrite that narrative, obviously, because how could I call myself the Poster Girl for Contentment if I hadn't?

On a recent trip, I was admiring the beautiful guest bedroom I'd been lucky enough to occupy during my stay at a friend's house. And here is how my thoughts progressed rapidly from gratitude and appreciation to shame:

"What a lovely bedroom, perfectly furnished and decorated. What a blessing to have stayed here the past few days" which led to:

"This room she has for guests is nicer than my ACTUAL bedroom at home" which led to:

"I'd have a better house if I'd made more money over the past few years" which led to:

A rush of shame and me spiraling with it, remembering jobs that I'd quit abruptly or moments I'd admitted another role wasn't working out.

In the midst of this swirl, I caught myself, took a deep breath and detached from the spiral. I began playing the new tape: I am content and successful, I deserve both things, and that none of that old stuff serves me. Worthiness is inherent. We don't have to hustle for it; we have it right now.

So, just to complicate the practice a bit, listen to the old narrative, and know it is embedded deep. Be patient with yourself. Rewriting it will take far longer than a week, but our intention is always the same: do what honors our contentment.

Don't look back,

Kim

Comparison Interrupts Flow

Worthiness. We left off with me sharing my story about shame spirals and how easily that pattern can re-emerge. I've learned to recognize when it's happening and name it for what it is. This is one of my management tools to keep me from getting mired. Learning about shame and self-worth has paid off beautifully in my life, and I recommend Brene Brown's "Gifts of Imperfection" to better understand how feeling worthy lets us live wholeheartedly.

For our practice, I want to clarify what worthiness is - and what it isn't. We need to expect good things in our lives and not feel guilty when we get them. Our expectations should be high, but they also need to be realistic. Contentment is something attainable. Enough is enough. The story we write is one of deserving contentment, but it isn't greedy. It isn't, "I'm worthy of contentment, so where is my fame and fortune?"

Making comparisons between our lives and those of others will trip up contentment every single time. Yes, we deserve good in our lives, but it's not about striving for more, more, more because we deserve everything. We can work toward what we want, while being content right now, exactly as things are. That's the power.

Like listening to our body, focusing on the story and keeping it centered on contentment will become intuitive with practice. Keep your expectations contentment-focused at all times. It's a Poster Girl Habit that keeps me flowing and one I want you to carry.

*Feel worthy *and* be realistic,*

Kim

Elevator Pitch

We are closing in on the end of our focus on the second habit, EXPECTATION. This phase of the practice has been devoted to the story we tell ourselves. We've listened in on our self-focused conversations. It's not eavesdropping - they're our thoughts and we SHOULD listen in!

Once we identified them, we started to challenge the automatic thoughts we have about ourselves. This is ongoing. As I shared, I still have to do this every day to make sure my contentment isn't interrupted.

We made a new commitment to tracking patterns: watching when we fall out of contentment flow and nothing the thoughts going on when it occurs. We have made an equal pledge to re-write and replace the old story with a new one that serves contentment.

Before we wrap up, we're going to do another exercise. This one is written, so use the dot-grid page opposite this one. If you don't like writing in your books, I understand. I'm that person, too. If you don't want to write in your Contentment Creation Guide, use a journal, a notebook, or the back of an old piece of junk mail.

Write down the "elevator pitch" version of the story of what you expect and deserve in life. Don't just write "I will be content" and end there (though that's a pretty powerful story unto itself!)

Take a few minutes and write out a pitch about who you are, what you deserve, and how you expect to receive it day by day. Write it, read it, re-read it. Write it over and over like Bart Simpson writing on the blackboard if it helps.

Here's mine: I'm Kim. I'm kind-hearted and observant. I'm a natural encourager. I am worthy of contentment. I enjoy my life!

How about you?

Pitch it until it's easy,

Kim

Bringing It All Together

This brings us to the end of the introduction to Habit Two, EXPECTATION, so let's bring it all together.

EXPECTATION refers to our mind and its focus, which comes from the story we tell. We are striving to experience LIGHTNESS OF MIND by practicing it.

Often we've been telling an old story for so long that it's automatic, nearly invisible, hard to separate. An example that gets used is the sky and the clouds painted across it. We are so used to seeing them together, they seem like one thing, but they aren't.

The EXPECTATION sub-habits are as follows:

❯ Surveillance - This means being vigilant and paying attention when your mind shifts. This will help you play detective. Watch yourself to see what thoughts come up as you fall out of flow, and build the habit of catching it early.

❯ Avoiding Shame Spiral - Here we are doing just that, staying out of the spiral. We catch the old automatic tapes in their early moments and rewind before a spiral happens. I shared a recent example from my life. It's easier to get out of a spiral if you see it coming on, just like taking medicine at the first sign of a migraine.

❯ Rewriting - This is the KEY to building this habit. Change your thoughts, change your life. Begin telling a new story and tell it over and over (and over). You are always listening to your thoughts, even when you don't realize it. The more your story is that you expect to be contented, the more contented you will feel.

To new, better stories,

Kim

Easy Delights

Introducing the Habit: Easy Delights

Habit #3 is EASY DELIGHTS, and its outcome is BRIGHTNESS OF MOOD. This is my favorite part of our practice together, because it's just so much fun.

EASY DELIGHTS are tiny bursts of magic. They are little mood brighteners hiding in plain sight. My classic example is seeing small birds (usually finches) that frequent sidewalks and parking lots. They hop! They chirp! They splash in puddles!

The examples are nearly endless, but the point is always the same. As you discover them, you're part of the process of creating them. Your decision to identify an EASY DELIGHT changes the energy of the moment and of your mood.

We just finished working through EXPECTATION, or telling ourselves a story that leads toward contentment. I expect to be contented, but do you know what else I move through the world expecting? I expect to be delighted. Let me tell you more about what I mean, and it will help set the stage for us to practice EASY DELIGHTS.

The main contentment role model in my life was my Gram, who was "easily delightable." It did not take much to delight her. She took bits of joy from the small stuff, everywhere and all the time. She appreciated what was pretty, unique, cute, or whimsical. In retrospect, it's easy to see why she enjoyed her life so much. She focused her lens on delightfulness all around her. It's around us, too.

As we focus on EASY DELIGHTS in their many forms, I'll give you examples from my collection and tips to start your own. It's all about noticing and appreciating, and it's amazing what this adds to our contentment practice.

We started from bodies that feel good and moved to minds that feel light, clear from clouds of negative thoughts. ENERGY was the foundation and EXPECTATION was the framing. Gathering EASY DELIGHTS is like furnishing the house, so to speak, and filling in any gaps in our contented Poster Girl flow.

Start Your Collection,

Kim

Be Easily Delightable

Being easily delightable makes you delightful.

Choosing this path, embracing the Poster Girl Habit of seeking EASY DELIGHTS, makes you a more contented, enjoyable person. It will open up space in your life where you may previously have shown up as grumpy, stressed, or self-involved. The spirit you bring when you're delighted changes the quality of all your interactions. It shifts your entire aura. I know, because it shifted mine.

Today, we are going to start collecting EASY DELIGHTS. If you've been wondering since yesterday, they are the stereotypical "little things", the everyday joys. They are sights, sounds, tastes, colors, textures. They are moments, funny interactions, sweet or touching gestures. EASY DELIGHTS are micro-experiences, and when you start to actively collect them, you will retrain your brain to look for them.

In the same way that keeping a gratitude journal tunes you into the presence of things to be grateful for, keeping a collection of EASY DELIGHTS tunes you in as well. Scarcely an hour of my waking life passes without me identifying some kind of EASY DELIGHT or another.

As we flow, I'll share some of my most common ones, and encourage you to collect and take note of your own. Then we will complete two exercises to cement EASY DELIGHTS as a habit that is second nature.

My easiest delights are birds and wildflowers, caterpillars and bumblebees. I delight in funky coffeehouse furniture, pretty mugs, pottery, latte art, baked goods. I like patterns and symmetry, muted colors and bright ones. The examples are endless. The habit is in seeking them all the time, in all situations, and allowing them to brighten your mood as you do.

Be a Collector,

Kim

Spirit + Skill

The first part of the EASY DELIGHTS habit is the spirit of it: Be Easily Delightable. Be willing to let things amuse and enchant you. Open up to delight. Welcome it in.

The second part of EASY DELIGHTS is the skill, what you need to actually DO to practice the habit. The skill is Noticing. This is an important and challenging part of the habit. We are all so busy, busy, busy with our lives, our jobs, our smartphone scrolls. We live in our heads in a way that can make the Noticing tricky.

As I mentioned yesterday, one of my main Easy Delights comes in the form of wildflowers. I love to take note of flowers and wild blooming plants on my daily walk. I love the different shapes of ferns and texture of mosses. I love the incredible range of shades of green - who knew? Well, I didn't know, for many years. Do plants come in more shades of green now? No, but I am awakened to them. I practice noticing by staying in the moment and looking for delights, almost like it's my job.

Noticing requires minimizing distractions, ones from inside of you and outside of you. The first two habits of ENERGY and EXPECTATION - these help quiet the noise or "chatter" from our bodies and minds. The distractions outside ourselves - stressors, electronics, even loved ones - managing those is another layer of challenge, but it can be done.

I've said often in my writing that my fasting practice helped make me a Noticer. This is true, because dialing down the volume of food noise and digestive disturbance brings on a special kind of quiet. Fasting also played a big role in quieting things by helping me manage my self-talk. Fasting is powerful but any can become a Noticer if they are determined to do so, regardless of eating pattern.

For today, practice the skill of Noticing. You don't even have to try to be delighted, just look and listen with more intention. What you see just might surprise you, so take as much notice as possible.

Combining spirit and skill,

Kim

Delights Of All Kinds

Classifying EASY DELIGHTS isn't the point, but knowing the wide range of kinds gives perspective. To illustrate, here's something I wrote it for my blog about a July 2019 trip to Myrtle Beach. It highlights the range of my EASY DELIGHTS and the effects they can have on mood. Read on - There are so many KINDS of easy delights.Easy Delights Are:

TEXTURAL - Frilly Spanish moss draped on trees like a feather boa. Dark green leaves on a magnolia tree so shiny, they seem to have been waxed.

COLORFUL - Flowering trees like the crepe myrtle. The shades of pink and yellow in the sky as the sun comes up.

WHIMSICAL - Choosing a special Tervis tumbler or can coozie to coordinate with your beach towel

SOOTHING - Listening to the waves crashing against the shore. The feel of clean sheets after a long day.

SILLY - Children digging holes on the beach and bringing water from the ocean one dump truck at a time. A crazy energetic spaniel who does not stop running in circles for the course of an entire long conversation by the humans.

RITUALISTIC - Coffee on the balcony in the same grass-green cup, seated on the same tall patio chair.

CONTRASTING - Icy cold air conditioning vs a hot humid afternoon. An invigorating shower to wash off the salt, sand and sweat.

ABSURD - An annoyed squirrel glaring at us in disdain. Someone catching a tiny shark right next to a "No fishing for sharks" sign (he threw it back).

TIMELESS - Sunrises and sunsets that look like they did a day ago, a year ago, a century ago

PLEASURABLE - Spicy pimento cheese on crunchy bagel crisps. A cold, fruity daiquiri. A basket of fresh bread with real butter. The fizz of champagne. Hot, tender baked potatoes. Carrot cake with cream cheese icing. OK, food is among the easiest of the delights!

GROUNDING - Being in a new place but having my husband right there. Knowing "home" is always right where you left it. Fasting through the bulk of the day for simplicity and clarity.

I could go on and on (I do!) but the point is not what I notice as EASY DELIGHTS, but what YOU notice them to be. You've embraced the spirit of it, you're practicing the skill of it, and your Collection has begun. Now, we expand and deepen the practice.

To delights of all kinds,

Kim

Collecting Has Its Benefits

The decision to include EASY DELIGHTS in this practice took a step of courage on my part, because for every person who has lit up about it, there's another who finds it silly or frivolous. Nonetheless, I am convinced to my marrow that collecting EASY DELIGHTS has a major benefit: contentment. How could I leave it out?

Now, we're going to start the EASY DELIGHTS collection as more of an actual "thing." Whether virtual or action, your Collection is a sort of photo album.

It can be virtual photo album (Facebook, Instagram or another electronic format). I post to Instagram, which shares to Facebook, so I have collected EASY DELIGHTS in both.

If you're really motivated, it could be an actual photo album, even an old-school scrapbook.

It can be a journal or blog where you document your EASY DELIGHTS in writing, lists or short paragraphs describing them. This would overlap very nicely with a gratitude journal practice.

OR, as I often do, you can start compiling a mental photo album, a collection of mental images. This is an inherently minimalist practice - there is no expense involved. There are no supplies, so there's no resulting clutter.

The most important aspect of collecting is that you maintain a virtual, running collection in your heart and mind each day, every day. These are to create a distinct brightness of mood, a strong layer that supports contentment.

When you look at your cumulative mood as the day goes on, it will correlate to the virtual collection you've been curating on a given day. If you have been intentionally amassing EASY DELIGHTS, you will find that your mood is brighter than if you have not.

When the day is done, you can let most of the EASY DELIGHTS go - after all, each day is the start of a fresh new collection!

To brightness of mood,

Kim

Scavenger Hunt in Tough Spots

In tough situations, on difficult days or just plain bad ones, the EASY DELIGHTS habit can lose some charm. Noticing them can seem frivolous in the face of life's more challenging experiences.

Thus, on the very worst of days, the Habit needs to be put on the back burner (or a high shelf for later retrieval). However, on a run-of-the-mill bad day, I invite you to put a little *extra* into the EASY DELIGHTS part of your practice.

Why? Because when many factors are conspiring to bring you out of flow, that's when you need contentedness the most. This is where contentment is something we've cultivated inside as a kind of emotional immune system.

So this exercise is called "Sucky Situation Scavenger Hunt." Today, in an annoying or boring part of your day, seek out EASY DELIGHTS in the midst of it all. They're there, I swear! Look for them, even if you have to look a little harder. And if today goes so smoothly that you can't practice the exercise, do it on a day very soon.

This is not to make light of the dark, heavy days of our lives. When you are struck by the traumas or unthinkable news, nobody expects you to look for a quirky detail to make you smile. But in the dentist's office - standing in a slow-moving line - in a boring staff meeting - or any day when you just feel low, blah, out of sorts - look for EASY DELIGHTS and let them brighten things.

It's important to see that not only can EASY DELIGHTS make good days great, but they can be deployed to make bad days better. That is what contentment is all about - staying in the flow, staying in the center, practicing the Habits.

Easy Delights are always there,

Kim

Bringing It All Together

This brings us to the end of the introduction to Habit Three, EASY DELIGHTS, so let's bring it all together.

I hope you're feeling a bit charmed by the idea of having EASY DELIGHTS as an intentional daily practice going forward. It brings BRIGHTNESS OF MOOD. There are moments when I wonder if I'm just a weirdo (no doubt about it, actually) but I've seen how EASY DELIGHTS resonate with people. It's a habit I've taught informally for months, and it's lingo that comes back over and over to confirm for me that others enjoy the practice and recognize its value.

The sub-habits of your EASY DELIGHTS practice are:

❯ The spirit of being easily delightable. This is a way of being, a framework for looking at the world, a "lens." The world is not more delightful than it was a few years ago. I simply choose to be more delightable than I was.

❯ The skill of being a noticer. This requires attentiveness, a deliberate minimization of internal and external distractions. This is a challenge, especially if you have a stressful job and/or caregiving duties. I wish I had been a Noticer when my children were small. I struggled to get out of my own head, but now that I'm out, I see clearly.

❯ Keeping an ongoing EASY DELIGHTS Collection, virtual or actual. I keep a little mental album running daily, and I document the best EASY DELIGHTS through digital photography.

❯ Scavenging for EASY DELIGHTS in tough moments. It's not a cure-all, but it helps keep the mood brightened, which supports overall contentment flow.

We built an ENERGY foundation, then an EXPECTATION frame, and now we've furnished the framework with EASY DELIGHTS. What's next? Habit #4, of course, which is EVERYDAY RITUALS and it will bring the decorative accents to go with our furnishings.

Wishing you the easiest of delights,

Kim

Everyday Rituals

Introducing the Habit: Everyday Rituals

The fourth Poster Girl Habit is what I call EVERYDAY RITUALS, and its outcome is DEPTH OF SATISFACTION.

What makes a set of behaviors qualify as a ritual? Why is Thanksgiving more than a bunch of people gathered around a dead bird? It's because of the intention and meaning attached to the behavior.

There is a difference between EASY DELIGHTS and EVERYDAY RITUALS. They're related but different in important ways. I know we've got a lot of E's going on here, but let's make sure we understand them each for their role and their benefits.

EASY DELIGHTS are little brighteners that we seek & find around us. They're already there. We don't need to create them, we only need to notice and appreciate them.

EVERYDAY RITUALS are patterns that we create and reinforce. They are behaviors we engage in, patterns to which we attach meaning. They won't exist unless we design and refine them. And in OUR Contentment Practice, they are a critical layer in keeping the flow.

The difference between life's big rituals like weddings, graduations, or holiday traditions is the ease and accessibility. EVERYDAY RITUALS are micro-rituals. We can create and practice them anywhere.

Next, we will discuss a little of the psychology behind WHY rituals matter.

Ritualize your flow,

Kim

Get Yourself Grounded

The power of rituals lies within repetition. My friend Laurie shared a ritual she recently took part in - the slow preparation of Turkish coffee with heated sand, copper pots, methodical pouring, and elegant serving. That's a ritual, but what makes a ritual in your own life is doing something intentionally and repeatedly.

There's deep human psychology that explains this power, how we are grounded and comforted by the familiarity of doing something the same way each day, each week, each month. In the ever-changing swirl of our lives, rituals come around and bring comfort.

The change of the seasons, the return of prom and graduation season, back to school, major holidays. They all have associated rituals that reassure us that as things change, others stay the same. While the world can seem chaotic, rituals bring a sense of power and control to our lives.

Rituals don't just provide safety, they bring satisfaction. The Swedish tradition of "Fika" is a word for having afternoon coffee and sweets, but I've heard it translated as 'a mini-paradise in the mid-afternoon'. Doesn't a daily dose of paradise seem like it could add contentment to your life?

In our practice of EVERYDAY RITUALS this week, we're going to talk about developing micro-rituals, small things you can do repeatedly to bring the power of rituals into every single day. Just because something isn't literally daily doesn't mean it won't qualify as an EVERYDAY RITUAL.

I have many small rituals that bring me satisfaction. Just like the one I described above, some of my main ones are around coffee, and though I may miss days here and there, they all qualify as EVERYDAY RITUALS.

Be thinking about a micro-ritual you already have, and if you can't identify a single one, be ready to create one.

In grounded, centered contentment,

Kim

Peaceful, Pleasurable, Productive

We are now working through the Habit #4, EVERYDAY RITUALS, which we've established are micro-rituals, meaningful yet accessible patterns we can repeat in our daily lives. I tend to sort them into three categories I call the 3 Ps: Peaceful, Pleasurable, and Productive. Here is a little bit more about what I mean:

Peaceful - These are quiet rituals that tend to be performed on our own: meditating, praying, journaling, reading a devotional, walking, or yoga. These are all rituals that invite peace, and they're all things I do at different times. My most common one is a long walk in nature, taken alone. Choosing one and doing it most days can create an EVERYDAY RITUAL.

Pleasurable - These are rituals that bring pleasure into life, and these are the ones that most often involve food and drink. Family gatherings, barbecues, potlucks, these can all be pleasurable rituals. They may involve the other senses, too, like hot baths, facials, massages. We anticipate them because of the pleasure they bring, and the more consistently we perform them, the deeper the satisfaction we derive.

Productive - These are micro-rituals, too - they are practiced consistently and with intention, but they also get stuff accomplished. Rituals around cooking, cleaning (I love laundry!), organizing, gardening, and canning can add the benefits of rituals AND make life easier. It's all about intentionality.

Many practices that make up this habit hit two of the three categories. Soon, I'll talk about my "signature EVERYDAY RITUAL", which hits all three points.

To the 3 Ps,

Kim

Take Yourself on a Date

In my second book, *Unmired*, I talk a little bit about rituals. Rituals are important to me. They mean so much that I've identified them as one of my five Poster Girl Habits for creating contentment. In *Unmired*, I describe a gratitude ritual I have around my latte. I'm going to talk more about it here, because it is a date I take myself on regularly.

Yes, I said latte - the large mug of espresso and steamed milk upon which talented baristas create artistic designs and images. My love affair with lattes in the last couple of years is what actually showed me the power of EVERYDAY RITUALS and caused me to intentionally design and develop new ones.

When I go to get my latte, the ritual begins on the drive toward the coffeehouse. I anticipate the latte. I start to feel happy and grateful while I'm parking the car and walking toward the building. I order my latte and watch the barista make it. I savor the whirring of the industrial espresso machine. I watch it being poured, finished off, and slid across the counter to me. I carry it to my seat and gaze upon it with my eyes. I smell it. I feel the warmth through the porcelain on both hands. I feel suffused with gratitude for the ritual, for the moment. And then, of course, I drink it!

When I am traveling and I get to visit a new town, I seek out a local coffeehouse to see what their decor and ambiance is like. And I order a latte, because even though it may be a bit different, the similarity in the ritual grounds and centers me.

This ritual is all 3 Ps - it's peaceful (I feel serene and contented in a coffeehouse), it's deeply pleasurable, and it's even productive. Since I practice daily fasting, I use this as a fast-breaking ritual to symbolically open my "eating window" most days.

You may not like lattes or drink coffee at all, but you can develop a meaningful EVERYDAY RITUAL that grounds your life the way this one grounds mine.

To deeply satisfying rituals,

Kim

Inviting Gratitude Flow

Now it's time to talk about Inviting Gratitude Flow.

Gratitude Flow is a state I've referenced frequently in my writing, but what does it mean? First, you set the stage, which means making some time to spend alone. I've done a lot of that over the past year, and I acknowledge that for many, it's more challenging to carve out the time than it is for me.

If you have a busy job with long hours or young children at home, it can be a real luxury to spend time by yourself, but it's an important part of developing Poster Girl Flow. Make it a priority as much as you're able so that you can invite Gratitude Flow.

Gratitude flow is a mind-body state. I can best describe it as being hyper-focused on feeling good. The better you feel, the more grateful you feel, and the two things enhance each other. A great way to start out would be to take yourself on a little date, something like the latte ritual I've described. Get into a grateful frame of mind enjoying the ritual, then build upon it.

I might go to the coffeehouse and enjoy my latte, then leave there feeling peaceful and content. From there, I might stroll to a nearby gift shop, looking at pretty stationery or pottery, collecting a few EASY DELIGHTS as I flow. Next I might move on to a walk around the neighborhood, looking at the landscaping and flower beds, watching a chipmunk darting across my path. This becomes meditative. It allows me to lose a sense of time and space, and keeps me free of thoughts beyond presence in the moment.

The gratitude amplifies until it becomes an expansive sense of freedom and joy inside. This is as good as it gets, folks! This is how my Poster Girl persona was born!

Inviting gratitude flow takes practice, but it's now a centerpiece of my contentment. Reflect on it and see if it resonates with you. The more consistently you stay in the flow, the easier it is to turn up the dial.

Invite more gratitude,

Kim

Design & Refine Rituals

Now it's time for your first EVERYDAY RITUAL. I'm going to ask you to choose a current ritual to refine/deepen, OR to design a brand-new one.

Think about what is realistic - an EVERYDAY RITUAL needs to be accessible without a lot of preparation or fuss. There shouldn't be a lot of additional supplies required. If you have a really creative idea, that's great - flow with it.

If you don't have immediate ideas, but you want to participate in practicing the habit, start with something easy. It doesn't have to be a coffeehouse latte. It can be any food or drink preparation process that you already do. Picking something pleasurable is an obvious choice!

Anything you do on a regular basis, especially if it is a daily thing, can be ritualized. It's all about the intention, the spirit in which you do it. Slow down, pay attention, be mindful, be grateful. Think about what may be missing, what could add depth. Fold in a new aspect that helps this ritual ground your life, as rituals are created to do.

Let's use tea as an example. Making tea is not just pouring water from a tea kettle into a teacup. It's anticipation of a wonderful experience. It's slowing down and savoring it while it lasts. Think about what your mid morning or afternoon tea means to you. Why are you drinking tea in the first place? Choose a favorite teal cup. Have a special saucer, a coaster, a doily, something that's a visual cue of the ritual. Prolong the entire process so that it starts to imprint on your mind as an EVERYDAY RITUAL.

It doesn't have to be tea - I don't happen to drink it. It's just letting ideas drift up. No pressure, no struggle, just flowing with it as it comes. There are no rules for the EVERYDAY RITUAL you're refining or designing. There is also no limit - you can practice several per week or even several per day. It's all about contentment and what invites more of it into your life.

To old and new rituals,

Kim

Bringing It All Together

This brings us to the end of the introduction to Habit FOUR, EVERYDAY DELIGHTS, so let's bring it all together.

EVERYDAY RITUALS are Habit #4 and they're performed to bring DEPTH OF SATISFACTION. These rituals are "mini" or micro-versions of big rituals like religious ceremonies, holiday traditions, and weddings. They are symbolic and they help ground us in the swirl of life's chaos.

Just as with the others, there are steps or sub-habits to internalize:

❯ We covered 3 main categories: Peaceful, pleasurable, productive, and some EVERYDAY RITUALS hit the marks to be included in two or even three.

❯ Solo rituals can be like taking yourself out on a date. EVERYDAY RITUALS can be done alone or with others, but there is a special satisfaction to ones that are completely self-focused.

❯ Performed consistently, EVERYDAY RITUALS can be an invitation to the state of Gratitude Flow. Gratitude Flow is induced by lining up EASY DELIGHTS and EVERYDAY RITUALS so they build on each other synchronistically.

❯ EVERYDAY RITUALS are not static things. Just like the bigger rituals in life that evolve as we flow, EVERYDAY RITUALS can and should be re-defined over time.

Up next is the fifth and final Poster Girl Habit: EDITING. Editing ensures that you always stay contented by empowering you to change what interrupts your contentment flow.

To satisfying rituals always,

Kim

Editing

Introducing the Habit: Editing

Just as I consider ENERGY the habit that runs underneath the entire practice, EDITING is the habit that "goes on top", overarching the practice like a roof. The outcome of EDITING is ENJOYMENT OF LIFE, and I don't have to tell you just how important that is. I seek to enjoy my life in honor of my grandmother's legacy, so my decisions are strongly influenced by doing what feels aligned with life enjoyment.

The process of EDITING is an ongoing self-inquiry, asking ourselves the questions to evaluate whether what we're doing in our lives working or not. It is a framework through which we can assess or "grade" our overall contentment flow. It is the hardest of the habits, but it's importance is truly paramount.

I use two guiding questions, and I'll say more as we continue practicing this habit. I look at an aspect of my life or a decision in front of me and I ask two questions, "Will this help me enjoy my life?" and "Does this feel like freedom?"

The answer to the question tells me the direction in which to flow. It tells me to move closer to a certain thing, or to move away from it. Envision a river flowing and branching - my guiding questions tell me which branch to flow down.

We will talk about how these questions can be used. They're useful for making choices like, "Should I eat this scone?" or "Should I fast through until this afternoon?"

Likewise, they can be used for the big stuff, questions like "Should I leave this job?" or "Should I stay in this relationship?" The consequences of making the "wrong" choice with a scone or a relationship can hardly be compared, but the process is the same. It's all about figuring out what keeps you in contentment flow and what takes you out of it.

To forever editing,

Kim

Continual Self Inquiry

EDITING is an important piece of the Poster Girl process because it's what keeps you from getting stuck and makes sure you continue to flow along. Before I developed the Habits, I was mired in struggle. All the Habits, especially EDITING, work to keep me unmired.

Using the guiding questions as previously described, we're going to build the habit of self-inquiry at the point of life's decisions. It's an ongoing inner dialogue that helps you choose whether to eat a cookie or stay up late. It also supports bigger decisions about relationships, family, and career.

I've made all of my decisions over the past couple of years by simply asking, "Will doing this thing help me enjoy my life?" If it's yes, I move toward it and if it's less clear, I pause. There is value in the pause, in not reacting impulsively. However, if it is a definite no, I'm out! I move swiftly away from all things (and people) that don't feel like freedom.

Currently, what questions do you ask yourself when you are in a decision-making mode? Do you ask yourself the questions calmly or in a bit of a ruffled panic? Reflect on this now. Assess your baseline attitude toward making changes in your life.

You may ask yourself what "makes sense." You may have a narrative about what's allowed based on your age or stage in life, or what your friends or colleagues expect of you. These are relevant issues to consider, of course, but if contentment is your central goal, it is important to look deeper within.

When the answer is Yes, it helps me enjoy my life and Yes, it feels like freedom, I have all the information I need for EDITING my life.

Next, we will begin the preliminary inventory and stake out the initial problem points.

Ask necessary questions,

Kim

Habit Inventory

Up next is a two-fold inventory-taking process: A Habit Inventory and then a Life Inventory. They are related but separate, so we will focus on the Habit Inventory first.

This is a process whereby, understanding the importance of practicing your Contentment Habits consistently, you "check in" on each of them. Since the Habits may be new to you, this may be your first round of checking in, but it's a great practice to develop.

ENERGY: How is your body feeling? Are you doing all the things that keep your foundation of feeling good intact? What's off track in this area for you?

EXPECTATION: What's the story you are telling yourself? Have you faltered at all in maintaining a narrative that expects contentment?

EASY DELIGHTS: Tell the truth, have you been letting them pass you by? Whenever we realize we've been seeing fewer of them, it's about inconsistency in our noticing. It's not because delight departed - they are always there. Make sure you are looking.

EVERYDAY RITUALS: Have you been slipping back into mindless patterns of behavior? The difference between an empty habit and a joyful ritual is the intention around it. Like the Habits themselves, you have to practice them to access their power.

This is the quick, easy Habit Inventory I've developed. I do it pretty much every week, checking in on how I feel and whether I'm consistently practicing the Habits that support my contentment. Next we'll talk about the Life Inventory, which is a more involved process - one you might only do every few months. When you feel off track, it's time for one....or both.

Inventory your habits,

Kim

Life Inventory

We just practiced EDITING by doing a Habit Inventory. That's something you should begin to do instinctively to make sure the Habits stay well-developed. This will keep you in flow. The first four Habits are internal, completely inside of you, so they have little to do with others. Contentment is individual and personal!

Now, we move our focus to performing a Life Inventory. What's the difference? This is a shift from looking at yourself and your mental/emotional practices to surveying your life globally. And ultimately, whenever anyone scans their whole life, the pain points stand out like a sore thumb. Most people can easily (if they're willing to be honest) point out what part of their life is the biggest barrier to contentment.

It might be your job (or conversely, staying at home when you'd prefer to be working.) It may be the type of house, the part of town, or the area of the country where you live. It may be a lack of friends or far too many so-called "friends" who don't show up for you.

It may be issues with your significant other or with your family of origin. These can be incredibly complicated and outside the scope of a workbook like this, but I encourage you to put in the time and effort to resolve them. I'm also unable via this book to make recommendations for seeking formal psychological treatment, but I know therapy can be helpful, especially if you have dealt with trauma in your history. It's not something I can help with, but I believe in you and I send love your way.

Before the next exercise, scan your life in your heart and mind. Identify a pain point that stands out at the top of the list. If you were urged to choose ONE aspect of your life standing between you and contentment, what would it be?

One edit at a time,

Kim

Ideal Day Comparisons

As a means of taking inventory in preparation for EDITING, we are going to revisit the "Ideal Day In The Future" exercise we looked at during Habit #1. Again, keep your eyes open and read, yet picture in your mind as you do.

We're going to envision an Ideal Day in your imagined future -maybe a few weeks or months down the road - and compare it against current reality.

In the ideal image, you wake up - where are you? In your current home, or is it a goal to move somewhere larger/smaller/different? Are you alone, with a partner, surrounded by family? These aren't always immediately "editable," but dwell on who wakes up under the same roof (or doesn't) and how it makes you feel. If there is a big disconnect between your ideal and what is current, make a note.

Do you drink coffee? Exercise? Meditate? Get dressed right away? What is the ideal morning routine for you, and how much does it look like what you actually do?

Are you spending the day at home or out in the world? What are you going to spend the bulk of this IDEAL day doing? If it's paid work, reflect on how the work you would do in your dream job compares to what you do in a typical day. If there is a big disconnect, there is a problem point here to note.

What about the later part of the day, your late afternoon and evening? What's the dinner plan? Who do you socialize with? Are you surrounded by family and friends who support your contentment? What rituals do you perform on an ideal day?

This visualizing supports the ongoing inventory of the EDITING habit. We have to know where our issues lie before we can address them. Most people who find their lives have drifted far from contentment have been failing to take inventory - or have been seeing the issues but haven't addressed them - yet.

We're preparing to discuss the empowerment part of editing - taking inventory, finding the issues, and becoming willing to take action to address them.

To days that mirror ideal,

Kim

Empowered to Edit Forever

Now we start to wrap up the fifth habit, EDITING, as we approach the end of our introduction to contentment practices. I want to encourage you to continue these habits long term. They are many years in the making for me, and they take longer than a few weeks to become deeply instinctual.

We envisioned an ideal day in the near future, and how a typical day may (or may not) differ from it. If there is no discrepancy between your ideal day and your typical one, you are nailing it. This is where contentment lies: knowing the kind of day and life you want, and living it in reality. I have finally arrived at this goal and I work every day to stay here.

Realistically, we all have an area (or a few) where we can make tweaks to get closer to our desired ideal. So ask yourself this: If you've identified something you need for ideal contentment and you aren't pursuing it, why? Truly look within. There's always a deeper reason why.

I understand that in terms of quitting a job or leaving a relationship, these are decisions to make carefully. There are serious consequences to those edits, and I'm not encouraging anyone to make rash moves. But I ask that you reflect on what stands between you and your contentment ideal.

We started in the early days of the ENERGY habit asking, "Is this a contentment-honoring choice?" You need to bring that same reflective spirit to decisions about where you live, what you do, and who gets your time and attention.

Do all these things honor your contentment? Only you know, so be empowered in EDITING if the answer is no.

To forever editing,

Kim

Bringing It All Together

This brings us to the end of the introduction to Habit FIVE, EDITING, so let's bring it all together.

EDITING keeps you in flow by steering your ship back on course when it veers. If you aren't in a state of contentment, if you aren't enjoying your life, then there are edits to be made.

❯ Asking the Guiding Questions

Mine are "Does this feel like freedom?" and, interchangeably, "Does this help me enjoy my life?" If these questions don't feel right, develop your own.

❯ Taking Inventory

Looking within and taking a sweeping overview of your life will show you instant sore spots if you're honest with yourself.

❯ Envisioning an Ideal Day in the Future

Dig deeper by regularly going through a guided imagery exercise called My Ideal Day in the Future.

❯ Making Comparisons

Once you know what your ideal day looks like, it's easier to see the differences between your current reality and that ultimate image.

❯ Choosing an Edit & Feeling Empowered

You have to start somewhere! Focus on an aspect of your life that needs change, and as you do, feel empowered, not apologetic. This is your life and your contentment is what's at stake.

This brings us to the end of this introduction to Poster Girl Habits, but it's only the beginning of your practice. Your own Contentment Practice will be ever-evolving and changing as your life flows where it's headed. I thank you for spending this time with me, and I hope you'll continue to follow the expansion of the program. Poster Girl Habits is my 2020 focus, and all updates will be at Unbelievable Freedom on Facebook, @unbelievablefreedom on Instagram, and of course, at www.unbelievablefreedom.com as well.

Wishing you contentment flow forever,

Kim

Made in the
USA
Middletown, DE